TIMOTHY FORSE

ELEVEN POINTS TO HEAVEN

Timothy Forse

ELEVEN POINTS TO HEAVEN

Poetic Reflections on the Christian Year and Life's Journey

To CB

Deo Gratias

2016

CONTENTS

Introduction and Explanation

The M 11.

There used to be No Services
So the sign said by the Motorway.
Now there are – and they are
A great convenience close to Stansted.
And yet so much time have I spent
In the to and fro between the two
Filling my mind with radio
Or a selected disc on the player.

Now I no longer drive it alone so much
I miss the pause for reflection
And dare to say some prayerful thoughts.
It replaced the services of Sunday Worship;
Compulsory Matins and Evensong of my youth
Voluntary Chapel and Compline as I grew
Then Holy Communion once confirmed.
I was told to wait a year for that
As I was too immature the Chaplain said.

And then I lost it all for a while.
No sense of purpose in my adolescence
My middle years marked by religious observance.
And then one day the door opened
I did that for him, and welcomed the guest
He came into my life, and stayed.

1.

Christmas Fair.

This is the night
At the heart of time
When love fulfilled the law.
The light of the life
That freely sets free
Any who seek and find.

This dawning light
Saving creation
Long after seven long days past
Came straight from heaven.
Born as a baby,
Manger bound He came.

Vulnerable as you and I
And more so
For his destiny an early death
A sinless sacrifice for sin
In exceptional exchange
Is now the source of Joy.

For this we celebrate
With coloured lights
And Christmas trees
And Seasonal Fairs
Glitter and festal gifts
We all have parties if we can.

We drink wine and more
And some is mulled
We bake extraordinary cakes
And greet more often
Hug and kiss more freely
And this is as a signal.

Awake from sleep
From darkness and December
Each year anew
Towards its end
A new Way begins
The Paradox perfected.

He is there if you will but look
And care for whom you greet
Help feed the hungry
The wounded, worn and world weary
Then will shine brightly
That fair light of Christmas

Come and adore him,
Love one another
Find him and peace
Beyond comprehension
And your sins forgiven
If you do but ask.

2.

New Year

Each time the year ends
With age, part of us dies within.
Better, in faith, something new begins.
Not only does this occur
On hearing Big Ben's twelfth stroke
Or the merry skirl of the bagpipes.
It is just most aptly celebrated
As we greet the New Year.

And yet at any moment
There is a freshness in following faithfully
That has the power to renew, then something new begins.
All of us can find this.
It is not just seeking the hero inside
It is the change of heart and mind
The transforming power for good
Which self searching then conversion brings.

This newness is the sign of joy revealed
The turning from those things that harm
And the hurt we feel and cause.
We cannot consciously convert this
Until we seek that pure Love
That is always waiting to be invited
Into the heart of each of us.
Knock, forgive and forgiven, come in and welcome.

3.

<u>Lenten Rose.</u>

Love comes afresh
With the first flower
Many different
For many nations

For Francis
The Almond blossom
The Southern Sign
Is first to appear

In England
The Primrose
And the Lenten Rose
Herald Him and the Spring

You are there
The metaphor tells
The sign of appearing
First you, Our Lord.

We follow, You forgive
Our faults and failures
Faced and absolved
Humans fit for healing

We can all fall
And fail again
Still you are there
To embrace and heal.

And with forgiveness
Wholenesss and grace
To make our Love
Complete.

Varese March 2015

On the Audience with Francis in front of St Peter's Basilica

7th March 2015

4.

Annunciation Eve.

This is the night
When God put right
The shame and blame
Of first Eve's blight

Gentle Mary
Source of Grace
Your Son announced
Our constant Light

Not as I will
But thine be done
Mary's Yes
Puts sin to flight

Her joy complete
When you are born
Grief pierced heart
When you depart

And now we know
As we believe
God with us
And you are He.

5.

<u>Easter 2015</u>

Christ is risen!
He is in the flowers of springtime
Bill promised on Good Friday
At his preaching of the Passion.
This is not the end.

The spring sunshine
Came out in time
To greet the Risen Lord
As the Paschal Mystery ended
And suddenly He is here.

Again, among us
In our meeting eyes
Handshakes and hugs
Now wreathed with smiles
The journey from sorrow ended.

And so we must
Go out with these
To tell the others
That were not there
He is unseen in each encounter

The Church is in such a state
Bill asked us twice
To respond Risen Indeed
The first half hearted
The second full meant

Francis is with Bill
He is there in the first flower
Wherever you are
You can begin again
The balm of mercy comes from Him.
To all of us if only we seek it.

6.

<u>Pentecost</u>

This is the day
We celebrate
The still small voice
That comes to some
As it were a flame
Surprising and unquenched.

To others
Horse Chestnut trees
Bloom natures candles
Bursting white
From cumulus clouds
Of green.

Now in England
Clear blue sky
Sun and softer air
Renew the Promise
God's gift to all
In light and sense.

Wherever you are
If two men in white
Ask "Why are you
Looking at the sky?"
Do not be lost
In wonder.

Say you are awaiting
The Saviour
Who will return
The Way he went
Then you must go out
To bring good news.

The gifts of love
And peace
Are hard to sense
By those hemmed in by hatred.
Yet share these gifts
With those we must.

For this is that love
The yearning strong
Beyond understanding.
It is outside ourselves,
And yet within.
The gift beyond price.

7.

The Feast of Corpus Christi.

We should not be surprised
Suddenly its summer.
The sun streams down
With fresh found warmth
That can bathe us all
In golden light.

And this is when
The heart celebrates
Perfect freedom
Every time
It turns towards
The source of love.

This is no less
Than that.
No single metaphor
Can ever fathom
The institution
Of His offering.

Thanks
Must be
Our response.
The celebration
From the heart
Of our witness.

Bread and wine
Transcending time
In spiritual food
His sacrifice
Complete.

Corpus Christi in England
Is known if at all
As a catholic ritual.
Just attend
Then find
The broken made whole.

8.

<u>Midsummer Love</u>

Midsummer comes
Fair grounds flourish,
The full bloom heady
With natural scent.
The sun never sets
North of the Circle.

Exams are sat,
Rejoicing follows.
Another generation
Graduates in life
From colleges
And all Nature's order.

This is the time
To be one
In thought and mind
Having compassion
For each other
Loving, courteous and kind.

That is easier
Said than done.
It is nonetheless
In the Good Book,

The First of Peter
To guide us.

Without this love
No other kind
Can flourish, neither
Parent for child or
Child honouring
Mum and Dad.

The same applies
Brother for sister
Girl for boy
Husband for wife,
Unless love flows
In each direction.

In any combination
The lack of love
Results in extremes
Of isolation
Possession or even
Suffocation.

We all deserve to know
When love flows
With the sense of

Joy in being,
Basking in the sun
Gazing at the stars.

That love which
Demands more or all
That has made
A song to sing
"Should I order cyanide
… or … champagne?"

This is of a different kind.
You know it
When it happens
Alright.
And we would not
Be here without it.

This love needs
The first love
To temper and
To balance it.

To build and grow
A reality when
New life and love
Can be safely born.

9.

Autumn Glory

September is the season
"Of mellow fruitfulness."

The sunlight softens
As natural gold radiates
And rose hips shake in the breeze.
The gathered harvest reminds the heart
Of completeness.

This is the time
For giving thanks
Contained in the Glory be
Where lips have shared
And hearts sustain
In silent fulfilment.

Our finite selves are transcended
He is the same, now and forever
And we are at one with Him
From age to age without end.

Barnham 21/09/2014

10.

<u>The Yes.</u>

I have walked among hills and ascended mountains
Gloried in the snow and swum in waters swift and still
Been bathed in sunshine refreshed by rain and more
Through all there is the thou.

There is the thou, the intimate you
Mankind is in danger of losing.
And I am glad to have found Him
In the way you came to me.

We all can find Him in the encounter
We have with each other
And yes it is in the gentle way
We touch each other.

This is not a sensual matter
As first it may be thought and felt
This is in the above and beyond
And even in faint hopes.

These are they that glimmer beyond despair
That strengthen souls in grief
And with healing time
Console the wounded and bereaved.

In the world where wellness
Is the goal much striven for
The thou may be unfashionable
And said to be from another age.

And yet it cannot be so,
This power that fashions us
There is no choice for the One
Invisible and yet at all times in all places.

Thou, the intimate you
Begins each day anew a dialogue
With each and every one of us
That seeks our response.

To clear the clutter and the clatter
That fills our lives so much
Is needed for us to hear
And then if we would but listen.

The Eve of All Saints. 2014

11.

Christ the King

Advent soon
Announces
His coming.
The suffering servant
Yet now becomes
Our King.

The second Coming
When God who is
Eternal felicity
Holds sway.
The King of Kings
And Lord of Lords.

We can now glimpse
The sacred diadem
Of Kingship on his brow.
This is the First
And the Last Word
In Governing.
Ultimately
One ruler
God the creator
Sustainer of life
Layer of foundations.

These are of Justice,
Mercy
And of Peace.
From whom
All Authority
Flows.

The Glory is
The Second Coming
When the Promise
Is fulfilled
When God will be all
In all.
And this is now
When me make it so.

21 11 15

Heaven.

Heaven is here, now and hereafter,
It is the gift within the Church
Above all pain
When we go
What will remain
Of us is Love.

Holding together
Those before us
With the gathered present
And those to come
Forming Communion
This is the Kingdom.

It is for us
To know and believe
For faith transcends
Time and place
It solves the why
Leaving only the when.

The answer is yes
It can when
The heart is found
By the encounter
With Another
"Ego sum. Noli timere."

Then suddenly
It is summer
In the soul.

The still small voice
Saying I am here
Do not be afraid
Reaches us, heals harms
Both now and forever
And here he is.

ABOUT THE AUTHOR

This is Tim Forse's first collection of Poetic reflections.

He has drawn his inspiration from a Community of Understanding of young people notably those belonging to the Communion and Liberation movement founded by Luigi Giussani.

This has taken him on a spiritual journey making increasing connection between the natural world and human experience within it.

It is rooted in his sacramental experience of being a regular communicant and the renewal process he has found in that.

The way he finds faith to illuminate reason is at one with the exposition provided by Luigi Giussani, and provides a path of understanding at once catholic and reformed.

8590236R00020

Printed in Germany
by Amazon Distribution
GmbH, Leipzig